I Remember

HELPING FAMILIES CONNECT
GOD'S WORD TO EVERYDAY LIFE

Nikki Greenfield

Illustrated by: Lou Wackes
Cover Design + Layout by: Alyssa Smith

FIRST EDITION

www.forgetfulandfierce.com

Dedicated to:

My super-hero husband— Adam

My incredibly awesome, fun, talented (and *sometimes* forgetful!) kids— Eden, Adam Jr., and Silas

All the *sometimes* forgetful children who will grow to remember Truth!

Dear Parents,

Family life is crammed with highs and lows... and lots of humdrum in-betweens! I hope this book will help your family thrive as you watch how the children on these pages connect God's Word to everyday life.

Use this as a point of connection for you and your child. Ask them questions as you read and look at the pictures. Define words for them. Pray that they would be reminded of these truths at just the right moments. On the next two pages you'll find more suggestions on how you can use this book to get the most out of it.

As this book enters your home, may God's grace and joy follow closely behind!

Happy Reading!
Nikki

Storybook

Although this book does not contain one continuous storyline, each page depicts a typical scenario that occurs in the real-life stories of many modern day kids. Read this book cover to cover to catch snapshots of difficult moments children face while growing up and the truths they can remember to overcome them.

Devotional

Instead of reading the entire book in one sitting, consider using it as a devotional resource. Go at a pace that works for your family. Read one scenario and coordinating scripture everyday ... or, more realistically, pick up the book every few days (or every few weeks... guilt-free!). Discuss it together as a family; or Mom or Dad can spend one-on-one time with each child for intentional discipleship at their level. Here are some suggestions to help you zero in on one page and apply God's Word to your child's life in a deeper way:

- Read each of the scriptures provided on the page.

- Show your child where they can find this scripture in their own Bible.

- Read the scripture along with its surrounding verses to bring greater understanding of the scripture's meaning and how it may relate to your child's life. (Particularly for older children.)

- Ask your child what this verse tells them about God. What does it tell them about themselves? How can it affect their choices today?

- Help your child memorize passages of scripture that are the most relatable to specific issues he/she is currently facing.

- Help your child memorize the, "I remember..." phrases, which can be helpful for when moments of temptation come. (Particularly for younger children)

- Ask your child questions like, "Have you ever felt this way?" And, "What can you remember the next time this happens?"

Conversation Starter

Don't worry about reading the text on the page! Flip through the book with your child, enjoy the artwork together, and ask questions that may trigger quality conversations.

- What do you see on this page?

- Does this remind you of anything?

- Can you relate to how the child in this picture may be feeling?

- Have you ever known anyone in this type of situation?

- What is your favorite page in this book? Why is it your favorite?

- Can you make up a name for the child in this picture? What do you think happened right before this? What will happen next?

- Do you remember what Bible verse goes along with this picture? Can you say it in your own words?

When the sun comes up and it's time to start the day,

I remember to be joyful!

"May the righteous be glad and rejoice before God;
may they be happy and joyful."
-Psalm 68:3

This is the
DAY
that the LORD
has made
we will
REJOICE
and be glad
in it.
– Psalm 118:24
ICB

When I have to kiss my parents goodbye
and go to class by myself,

I remember I am not alone!

Then Jesus came to them and said... "You can be sure
that I will be with you always." Matthew 28:18, 20 ICB

BE STRONG & COURAGEOUS. DO NOT be terrified, do NOT be discouraged, for the LORD your GOD will be with you ~ WHEREVER ~ you go.

Joshua 1:9

When someone is different from me or talks weird or smells funny or doesn't do things the way I would do them,

I remember to love!

"If God so loved us, we also ought to love one another."
- 1 John 4:11 ESV

Above
all else

Clothe yourselves
with **LOVE**
which binds us
ALL TOGETHER
in perfect
harmony.

—Col. 3:14
NLT

When someone hurts my feelings and I want
to say something mean,

I remember to build others up!

"When you talk, you should always be kind and wise."
-Colossians 4:6 ICB

"Encourage ONE ANOTHER and BUILD each other up."

I Thess. 5:11 NIV

When we're playing a game and my friend wants to go first,

I remember to let others be first!

"Don't look out only for your own interests, but take
an interest in others, too." -Philippians 2:4 NLT

Whoever
wants to be first
must take last place
and be the
SERVANT
of everyone
else.

Mark 9:35
NLT

When my friends come over to play and leave a big mess for me to clean up,

I remember to be neighborly!

"Do not neglect to do good and to share what you have, for such sacrifices are pleasing to God."
-Hebrews 13:16 ESV

SHOW hospitality to one another without Grumbling.

1 Peter 4:9 ESV

When my brother bites me, or my sister pulls my hair,
or my cousin breaks my favorite sword,

I remember to forgive!

"You, Lord, are forgiving and good, abounding in love
to all who call to you." -Psalm 86:5 NIV

Be... **TENDERHEARTED**

forgiving one another

as God in Christ

forgave you.

Ephesians 4:32 ESV

When my baby sister is just so cute that I want to squeeze her with all my might,

I remember to be gentle!

"Let all men see that you are gentle and kind."
-Philippians 4:5 ICB

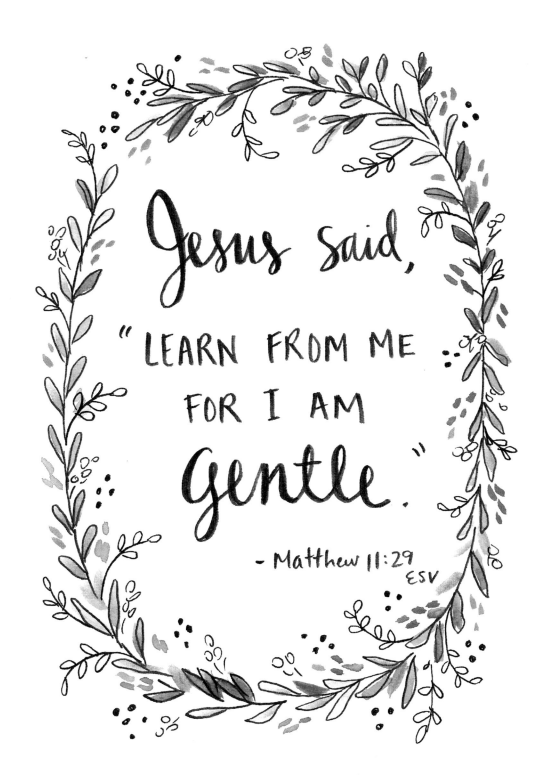

Jesus said,

"LEARN FROM ME
FOR I AM
Gentle."

- Matthew 11:29
ESV

When I have to clean my room,
I remember to not complain!

"Whatever you do, work at it with all your heart."
- Colossians 3:23 NIV

DO
EVERYTHING
~~without~~
complaining
or
arguing.

Phil. 2:14
NLT

When I want to yell or throw something or hit someone or steal candy out of the cabinet or sneak frosting off the birthday cake,

I remember to control myself!

"…encourage the young men to be self-controlled."
-Titus 2:6 NIV

BETTER
to have
Self-Control
than
TO CONQUER
A CITY.

Proverbs 16:32
NLT

When I absolutely, completely, and totally do NOT
want to share the new toy I got for my birthday,

I remember to be generous!

"The godly are generous givers." -Psalm 37:21 NLT

Give to the one who asks you and do not turn away from the one who wants to borrow from you.

Matthew 5:42
NIV

When I don't want to run errands with Mom and I don't like my dinner and I am having the worst day in the world,

I remember to be thankful!

"And whatever you do, in word or deed, do everything in the name of the Lord Jesus, giving thanks to God the Father through him." -Colossians 3:17 ESV

GIVE
Thanks
in all
Circumstances

I Thess. 5:18 ESV

When I feel lazy at chore time or my homework seems too hard,

I remember that God made me to be a hard worker!

"Anyone too lazy to cook will starve, but a hard worker is a valuable treasure." -Proverbs 12:27 CEV

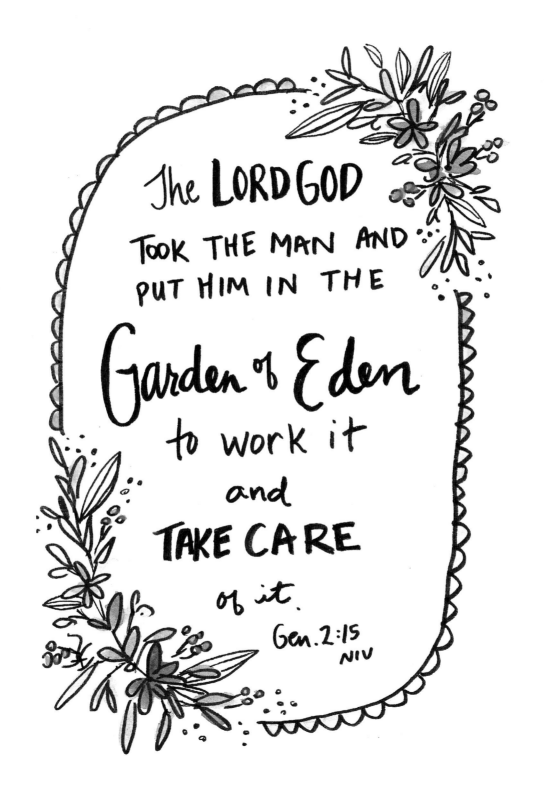

The LORD GOD TOOK THE MAN AND PUT HIM IN THE Garden of Eden to work it and TAKE CARE of it.

Gen. 2:15
NIV

When Mom says it's time for a bath or Dad says
to turn off the device and I just don't want to,

I remember to obey!

"Children, obey your parents in the Lord, for this is
right." -Ephesians 6:1 ESV

I WILL HURRY without delay to OBEY your commands.

Psalm 119:60 NLT

When I feel afraid at night in my bed,
I remember that God is watching over me!

"The Lord keeps you from all harm and watches over your life." -Psalm 121:7 NLT

The LORD is
with me; I will not
be AFRAID.
The LORD is
with me; he is my
HELPER.

Psalm 118:6-7 NIV

Made in the USA
Columbia, SC
20 May 2019